contents

NZ, Canada, US and UK readers
Please note that Australian cup and spoon
measurements are metric. A quick conversion
guide appears on page 63.

marinated bocconcini

2 tablespoons olive oil
1 fresh long red chilli, chopped finely
1 tablespoon finely chopped fresh
  flat-leaf parsley
1 tablespoon finely grated lemon rind
12 bocconcini (720g), halved
2 tablespoons lemon juice

Combine oil, chilli, parsley and rind in medium bowl; add cheese, toss to coat in marinade. Cover; refrigerate 3 hours or overnight.
Drain cheese mixture, drizzle with juice and serve with lemon wedges, if desired.

serves 4
per serving 36g fat; 1886kJ (452 cal)

orange and oregano marinated olives

600g large green olives, drained
3 orange slices, quartered
5 sprigs fresh oregano
1 cup (250ml) olive oil
½ cup (125ml) orange juice
2 teaspoons black peppercorns

Layer olives, orange and oregano into hot sterilised 1-litre (4-cup) jar.
Gently heat oil, juice and peppercorns in small saucepan. Pour enough of the oil mixture into jar to cover olives completely, leaving 1cm space between olives and top of jar; seal while hot.

makes 4 cups
per tablespoon 2.9g fat; 141kJ (35 cal)
tips Best made 3 days ahead.
Can be refrigerated up to 3 weeks; serve at room temperature.

roast tomatoes with garlic crumbs

6 large egg tomatoes (540g)
2 teaspoons balsamic vinegar
1 teaspoon caster sugar
2 tablespoons olive oil
1 clove garlic, crushed
½ cup (35g) stale breadcrumbs

Preheat oven to hot (220°C/200°C fan-forced).
Halve tomatoes lengthways; place, cut side up, on lightly greased ovenproof dish. Brush with vinegar; sprinkle with sugar. Bake about 20 minutes.
Heat half of the oil in small saucepan; cook garlic and breadcrumbs, stirring, about 4 minutes or until crumbs are golden brown. Serve tomato sprinkled with garlic crumbs and drizzled with remaining oil.

serves 4
per serving 9.6g fat; 568kJ (136 cal)

pan-fried asparagus with parmesan

1 tablespoon olive oil
400g asparagus, trimmed
½ cup (40g) flaked parmesan
½ teaspoon cracked black pepper

Heat oil in large frying pan; cook asparagus, in batches, until just tender.
Serve asparagus sprinkled with cheese and cracked pepper.

serves 4
per serving 7.9g fat; 424kJ (101 cal)

beef carpaccio with rocket, parmesan and aïoli

Carpaccio is to the Italians what sashimi is to the Japanese. Usually served as an appetiser, the delicately sliced raw beef fillet is commonly served drizzled with olive oil and lemon juice.

400g piece beef fillet, trimmed
80g wild rocket leaves
100g parmesan, shaved
aïoli
1 egg
1 clove garlic, quartered
1 tablespoon lemon juice
1 tablespoon dijon mustard
½ cup (125ml) olive oil

Wrap beef tightly in plastic wrap; place in freezer about 1 hour or until partially frozen.
Meanwhile, make aïoli.
Using sharp knife, slice unwrapped beef as thinly as possible; arrange beef on serving plate.
Top beef with rocket and cheese; drizzle with aïoli.
aïoli Blend or process egg, garlic, juice and mustard until combined. With motor operating, add oil in a thin, steady stream until aïoli thickens slightly.

serves 4
per serving 41.8g fat; 2134kJ (510 cal)

salami, potato and basil frittata

2 medium potatoes (400g), sliced thinly
250g sliced Italian salami
6 eggs, beaten lightly
½ cup (125ml) cream
3 green onions, chopped coarsely
1 tablespoon finely shredded fresh basil

Preheat oven to moderate (180°C/160°C fan-forced).
Grease deep 20cm-round cake pan; line base and side
with baking paper.
Boil, steam or microwave potato until just tender. Drain; cool.
Cook salami in small heated non-stick frying pan, stirring, until
browned all over; drain on absorbent paper.
Layer half of the potato over base of pan; top with half of
the salami. Repeat with remaining potato and salami. Pour in
combined egg, cream, onion and basil; bake, uncovered, about
30 minutes or until firm. Frittata can be served warm or cold.

serves 4
per serving 45.1g fat; 2349kJ (562 cal)
tip Can be made a day ahead and refrigerated, covered.

olive, anchovy and caper bruschetta

½ loaf ciabatta (275g)
3 cloves garlic, halved
⅓ cup (80ml) olive oil
3 anchovy fillets, drained, chopped finely
½ cup (60g) seeded black olives, chopped finely
1 tablespoon drained baby capers
1 tablespoon lemon juice
⅓ cup (25g) flaked parmesan
2 tablespoons fresh marjoram leaves

Preheat grill.
Cut ciabatta into 1.5cm-thick slices; halve any large slices crossways. Toast under hot grill until browned lightly; while still hot, rub one side of toast with garlic. Place, in single layer, on tray; drizzle ¼ cup (60ml) of the oil evenly over toast.
Combine anchovy, olives, capers, juice and remaining oil in small bowl.
Just before serving, divide olive mixture among bruschetta; top with cheese, then marjoram.

serves 8
per serving 11.7g fat; 857kJ (205 cal)
tip Ciabatta can be prepared 3 hours ahead. Make and top with olive mixture just before serving.

suppli al telefono

This delicious snack from Italy originally got its name from the strings of melted mozzarella that resemble telephone wires when the balls are pulled apart. You need to cook about ⅓ cup of rice for this recipe.

1 tablespoon olive oil
⅓ cup (40g) frozen peas
2 cloves garlic, crushed
1 cup cooked white medium-grain rice
⅓ cup (25g) finely grated parmesan
1 egg, beaten lightly
1 tablespoon coarsely chopped fresh oregano
40g mozzarella
½ cup (35g) stale breadcrumbs
vegetable oil, for deep-frying

Heat olive oil in large frying pan; cook peas and garlic until peas are just tender and garlic is fragrant.
Combine pea mixture in medium bowl with rice, parmesan, egg and oregano. Using hands, shape rice mixture into eight balls.
Cut mozzarella into eight cubes. Press a hole into the middle of each ball; insert a piece of mozzarella, then re-mould rice to cover hole. Roll balls in breadcrumbs to coat all over.
Heat vegetable oil in large saucepan; deep-fry balls, in batches, until browned lightly and heated through.

makes 8
per ball 9.9g fat; 621kJ (148 cal)

spaghetti napoletana

2 x 400g cans whole peeled tomatoes
30g butter
1 tablespoon olive oil
2 cloves garlic, crushed
1 tablespoon shredded fresh basil
2 tablespoons chopped fresh flat-leaf parsley
250g spaghetti

Push tomatoes, with their liquid, through sieve.
Heat butter and oil in large saucepan; add garlic, cook, stirring,
1 minute. Add pureed tomato; bring to a boil. Reduce heat;
simmer, uncovered, about 40 minutes or until sauce reduces
by about half. Stir in basil and parsley.
Meanwhile, cook pasta in large saucepan of boiling water until
tender; drain. Combine sauce and pasta.

serves 2
per serving 23.6g fat; 2750kJ (658 cal)

penne puttanesca

500g penne
⅓ cup (80ml) extra virgin olive oil
3 cloves garlic, crushed
1 teaspoon chilli flakes
5 medium tomatoes (950g), chopped coarsely
200g seeded kalamata olives
8 anchovy fillets, drained, chopped coarsely
⅓ cup (65g) rinsed drained capers
⅓ cup coarsely chopped fresh flat-leaf parsley
2 tablespoons finely shredded fresh basil

Cook pasta in large saucepan of boiling water, uncovered, until just tender.
Meanwhile, heat oil in large frying pan; cook garlic, stirring, until fragrant. Add chilli and tomato; cook, stirring, 5 minutes. Add remaining ingredients; cook, stirring occasionally, about 5 minutes or until sauce thickens slightly.
Add drained pasta to sauce; toss gently to combine. Serve sprinkled with small basil leaves, if desired.

serves 4
per serving 21.2g fat; 2822kJ (674 cal)

lasagne bolognese

2 teaspoons olive oil

6 slices pancetta (90g), chopped finely

1 large white onion (200g), chopped finely

1 medium carrot (120g), chopped finely

1kg beef mince

2 cups (500ml) beef stock

1 cup (250ml) dry red wine

2 x 410g cans tomato puree

2 tablespoons tomato paste

¼ cup finely chopped fresh flat-leaf parsley

250g fresh lasagne sheets

2 cups (160g) finely grated parmesan

white sauce

125g butter

¾ cup (110g) plain flour

1.25 litres (5 cups) hot milk

Heat oil in large heavy-based pan; cook pancetta, stirring, until crisp. Add onion and carrot; cook, stirring, until vegetables soften. Add beef; cook, stirring, until beef just changes colour. Add stock, wine, puree and paste; simmer, uncovered, 1½ hours. Remove from heat; stir in parsley.

Meanwhile, make white sauce.

Preheat oven to moderately hot (200°C/180°C fan-forced). Grease deep 26cm x 35cm baking dish.

Spread about ½ cup of the white sauce over base of dish. Layer two pasta sheets, ¼ of the bolognese sauce, ¼ cup of the cheese and about 1 cup of the remaining white sauce in dish. Repeat layering process, starting with pasta sheets and ending with white sauce. Top lasagne with remaining cheese.

Bake, uncovered, about 40 minutes or until top is browned lightly. Stand 15 minutes before cutting.

white sauce Melt butter in medium saucepan, add flour; stir until mixture forms a smooth paste. Gradually stir in milk; bring to a boil, stirring, until sauce thickens.

serves 8
per serving 53.1g fat; 3657kJ (874 cal)

fettuccine boscaiola with chicken

The pasta sauce known as boscaiola translates roughly as woodcutter's sauce, a name thought to have evolved from the fact that Italian woodsmen made good use of the fungi harvested from beneath the trees they felled, back at their campfire at night. You need about half a large barbecued chicken for this recipe.

500g fettuccine
1 tablespoon olive oil
1 medium brown onion (150g), chopped finely
2 bacon rashers (140g), chopped finely
200g button mushrooms, sliced finely
¼ cup (60ml) dry white wine
⅔ cup (160ml) cream
1 cup (250ml) milk
1 cup (170g) thinly sliced cooked chicken
¼ cup (20g) finely grated parmesan
2 tablespoons coarsely chopped fresh flat-leaf parsley

Cook pasta in large saucepan of boiling water, uncovered, until just tender; drain, reserving ½ cup of cooking liquid.
Meanwhile, heat oil in large saucepan; cook onion, stirring, until soft. Add bacon and mushrooms; cook, stirring, 1 minute.
Add wine, cream and milk; bring to a boil. Reduce heat; simmer, stirring, 5 minutes. Add chicken; stir until combined.
Add pasta, parmesan, parsley and reserved cooking liquid; toss gently over low heat until hot.

serves 4
per serving 32.9g fat; 3425kJ (818 cal)
tip Fresh basil can be used instead of parsley, if you prefer.

19

spaghetti marinara

1 tablespoon olive oil
1 medium brown onion (150g), chopped finely
⅓ cup (80ml) dry white wine
⅓ cup (95g) tomato paste
2 x 425g cans whole peeled tomatoes
750g seafood marinara mix
¼ cup coarsely chopped fresh flat-leaf parsley
375g spaghetti

Heat oil in large frying pan; cook onion, stirring, until soft.
Add wine, paste and undrained tomatoes to pan; bring to a
boil. Reduce heat; simmer, uncovered, 10 minutes or until
sauce thickens slightly.
Add marinara mix; cook, stirring occasionally, about 5 minutes
or until seafood is cooked through. Stir in parsley.
Meanwhile, cook pasta in large saucepan of boiling water,
uncovered, until just tender; drain.
Serve marinara sauce on top of pasta.

serves 4
per serving 11.2g fat; 2654kJ (635 cal)

herbed ricotta ravioli in tomato broth

⅓ cup (30g) finely grated parmesan
⅔ cup (130g) low-fat ricotta
1 tablespoon finely chopped fresh basil
2 tablespoons finely chopped fresh chives
24 wonton wrappers
16 medium egg tomatoes (1.2kg)
2 green onions, sliced thinly

Combine cheeses and herbs in small bowl. Place one rounded teaspoon of cheese mixture in centre of each of 12 wonton wrappers; brush around edges with a little water. Top each with a remaining wrapper, press around edges firmly to seal. Place ravioli on tray, cover; refrigerate 20 minutes.

Meanwhile, bring large saucepan of water to a boil. Place cored tomatoes in pan; return to a boil. Cook, uncovered, 2 minutes. Strain tomatoes over large bowl; reserve cooking liquid.

Blend or process tomatoes, in batches, until smooth; push through a food mill (mouli) or sieve into small saucepan; bring to a boil. Reduce heat; simmer, uncovered, 5 minutes.

Meanwhile, cook ravioli in large saucepan of reserved cooking liquid, uncovered, about 4 minutes or until they float to the surface; drain. Divide tomato broth and ravioli among serving bowls; sprinkle with onion.

serves 4
per serving 5.9g fat; 850kJ (203 cal)

gnocchi al quattro formaggi

Pasta with four cheeses is one of the most delectable (and among the richest!) of all the classic Italian sauces. Here, we team it with gnocchi, but it also marries well with fettuccine or tagliatelle.

¼ cup (60ml) dry white wine
1 cup (250g) mascarpone
1 cup (120g) coarsely grated fontina cheese
½ cup (40g) coarsely grated parmesan
¼ cup (60ml) milk
625g gnocchi
75g gorgonzola cheese, crumbled

Add wine to large saucepan; boil, uncovered, until wine reduces by half. Reduce heat, add mascarpone; stir until mixture is smooth. Add fontina, parmesan and milk; cook, stirring, until cheeses melt and sauce is smooth.
Meanwhile, cook gnocchi in large saucepan of boiling water, uncovered, until they rise to the surface and are just tender; drain.
Add gnocchi and gorgonzola to sauce; toss gently to combine.

serves 4
per serving 59.5g fat; 3294kJ (788 cal)

cheese and spinach tortellini with gorgonzola sauce

30g butter
2 tablespoons plain flour
1 cup (250ml) milk
¾ cup (180ml) cream
100g gorgonzola cheese, chopped coarsely
750g cheese and spinach tortellini
¼ cup loosely packed fresh flat-leaf parsley leaves

Melt butter in medium saucepan; cook flour, stirring, about 2 minutes or until flour bubbles and thickens.
Gradually stir in milk and cream; bring to a boil. Reduce heat; simmer, uncovered, until sauce boils and thickens. Remove from heat; stir in cheese.
Meanwhile, cook pasta in large saucepan of boiling water, uncovered, until just tender; drain.
Combine pasta with sauce; sprinkle with parsley and pepper.

serves 4
per serving 58.7g fat; 3699kJ (885 cal)
tips Ravioli or gnocchi can be substituted for the tortellini.
It's best to choose a ricotta-and-spinach-filled tortellini (or the even simpler ricotta-filled version) when making this sauce, as it doesn't marry overly well with meat-filled pastas.

chicken, pea and prosciutto risotto

3 cups (750ml) chicken stock
3 cups (750ml) water
10g butter
2 tablespoons olive oil
1 small brown onion (80g), chopped finely
2 cups (400g) arborio rice
½ cup (125ml) dry white wine
350g chicken breast fillets, chopped coarsely
2 cloves garlic, crushed
1½ cups (180g) frozen peas
6 slices prosciutto (90g)
2 tablespoons finely shredded fresh sage

Place stock and the water in large saucepan; bring to a boil. Reduce heat; simmer, covered.

Heat butter and half of the oil in large saucepan; cook onion, stirring, until soft. Add rice; stir rice to coat in mixture. Add wine; cook, stirring, until liquid is almost evaporated.

Stir in 1 cup simmering stock mixture; cook, stirring, over low heat until liquid is absorbed. Continue adding stock mixture, in 1-cup batches, stirring until absorbed after each addition. Total cooking time should be about 35 minutes or until rice is tender.

Meanwhile, heat remaining oil in medium frying pan; cook chicken, stirring, until cooked through. Add garlic; stir until fragrant. Stir chicken mixture and peas into risotto.

Cook prosciutto in same frying pan until crisp; drain on absorbent paper; break into pieces. Stir sage and half of the prosciutto into risotto; sprinkle remaining prosciutto over individual servings.

serves 4
per serving 18.8g fat; 2784kJ (666 cal)

osso buco with caper gremolata

8 pieces veal osso buco (2kg)
2 tablespoons plain flour
¼ cup (60ml) olive oil
1 medium brown onion (150g), chopped coarsely
2 cloves garlic, crushed
3 trimmed celery stalks (300g), chopped coarsely
2 large carrots (360g), chopped coarsely
2 x 400g cans crushed tomatoes
2 tablespoons tomato paste
1 cup (250ml) dry white wine
1 cup (250ml) beef stock

caper gremolata
1 tablespoon finely grated lemon rind
⅓ cup finely chopped fresh flat-leaf parsley
2 cloves garlic, chopped finely
1 tablespoon drained capers, rinsed, chopped finely

Toss veal in flour; shake away excess. Heat half the oil in large flameproof casserole dish; cook veal, in batches, until browned.
Heat remaining oil in same dish; cook onion, garlic, celery and carrot, stirring, until vegetables soften. Stir in undrained tomatoes, tomato paste, wine and stock.
Return veal to dish, fitting pieces upright and tightly together in single layer; bring to a boil. Reduce heat; simmer, covered, 2 hours. Uncover; cook about 30 minutes or until veal is almost falling off the bone.
Meanwhile, make caper gremolata.
Divide veal among serving plates; top with sauce, sprinkle with gremolata. Serve with soft polenta, if desired.
caper gremolata Combine ingredients in small bowl.

serves 4
per serving 19.9g fat; 2240kJ (536 cal)

veal marsala

2 tablespoons olive oil
4 veal leg steaks (500g)
1 medium brown onion (150g), chopped finely
250g button mushrooms, sliced thinly
¼ cup (60ml) marsala
⅔ cup (160ml) beef stock
1 tablespoon chopped fresh chives

Heat oil in large frying pan. Cook veal until browned
on both sides and cooked as desired; remove.
Add onion to same pan; cook, stirring, until soft.
Add mushrooms, marsala and stock; stir over heat
until mixture boils and thickens slightly.
Serve sauce over sliced veal; sprinkle with chives.
Serve with soft polenta, if desired.

serves 4
per serving 11.7g fat; 1268kJ (303 cal)

chicken cacciatore

2 tablespoons olive oil
1.5kg chicken pieces
1 medium brown onion (150g), chopped finely
1 clove garlic, crushed
½ cup (125ml) dry white wine
1½ tablespoons vinegar
½ cup (125ml) chicken stock
400g can diced tomatoes
1 tablespoon tomato paste
3 anchovy fillets, chopped finely
½ cup (60g) seeded black olives, halved
2 tablespoons chopped fresh flat-leaf parsley

Preheat oven to moderate (180°C/160°C fan-forced).
Heat oil in large frying pan; cook chicken until browned all over.
Place chicken in ovenproof dish.
Cook onion and garlic in same pan until onion is soft. Add wine
and vinegar; bring to a boil. Boil until reduced by half. Add stock,
undrained tomatoes and paste; bring to a boil.
Pour tomato mixture over chicken pieces. Cook, covered, in
oven 45 minutes.
Stir in anchovy and olives; cook, uncovered, 15 minutes.
Serve sprinkled with parsley.

serves 4
per serving 42.2g fat; 2571kJ (615 cal)

veal scaloppine with soft polenta

3 cups (750ml) water
1½ cups (375ml) chicken stock
1 cup (170g) instant polenta
½ cup (125ml) milk
½ cup (40g) finely grated pecorino cheese
12 veal steaks (960g)
80g butter
1 tablespoon lemon juice
2 tablespoons coarsely chopped fresh flat-leaf parsley

Bring the water and stock to a boil in large saucepan. Gradually stir in polenta; cook, stirring, until mixture thickens. Add milk and cheese; stir until cheese melts.
Meanwhile, heat a large oiled non-stick frying pan; cook veal, in batches, until browned on both sides and cooked as desired. Cover to keep warm.
Melt butter in same pan; stir in juice and parsley.
Divide polenta and veal among serving plates; drizzle with lemon and parsley butter.

serves 6
per serving 18.2g fat; 1714kJ (410 cal)

chicken, lemon and artichoke skewers

You need to soak 12 bamboo skewers in water for a least
30 minutes before use to prevent splintering and scorching.

2 tablespoons lemon juice
2 tablespoons olive oil
2 cloves garlic, crushed
2 medium lemons (280g)
500g chicken breast fillets, diced into 3cm pieces
2 x 400g cans artichoke hearts, drained, halved
24 button mushrooms (300g)

Place juice, oil and garlic in screw-top jar; shake well.
Cut lemons into 24 pieces. Thread chicken, artichoke,
mushrooms and lemon onto 12 skewers.
Cook skewers on heated oiled grill plate (or grill or barbecue)
until chicken is cooked through, brushing with juice mixture
while cooking.

serves 4
per serving 12.8g fat; 1170kJ (280 cal)

saltimbocca

Saltimbocca is a classic Italian veal dish that literally means "jump in the mouth", just the sensation the wonderful flavours will produce with your first bite.

8 veal steaks (680g)
4 slices prosciutto (60g), halved crossways
8 fresh sage leaves
½ cup (50g) finely grated pecorino cheese
40g butter
1 cup (250ml) dry white wine
1 tablespoon coarsely chopped fresh sage

Place steaks on board. Place one piece prosciutto, one sage leaf and one-eighth of the cheese on each steak; fold in half to enclose filling, secure with a toothpick or small skewer.
Melt half of the butter in medium non-stick frying pan; cook saltimbocca, in batches, about 5 minutes or until browned both sides and cooked through. Cover to keep warm.
Pour wine into same frying pan; bring to a boil. Boil, uncovered, until reduced by half. Stir in remaining butter, then chopped sage.
Divide saltimbocca among serving plates; drizzle with sauce and serve with risotto and steamed green beans, if desired.

serves 4
per serving 16.6g fat; 1517kJ (363 cal)

cioppino

This fish stew originated in San Francisco's large Italian fishing community.

2 uncooked crabs (700g)
16 uncooked large prawns (500g)
450g swordfish steaks
1 tablespoon olive oil
1 medium brown onion (150g), chopped coarsely
2 trimmed celery stalks (100g), chopped coarsely
3 cloves garlic, crushed
6 medium tomatoes (1kg), chopped coarsely
415g can tomato puree
½ cup (125ml) dry white wine
1⅓ cups (330ml) fish stock
1 teaspoon white sugar
200g clams, scrubbed
200g scallops
2 tablespoons finely shredded fresh basil
⅓ cup coarsely chopped fresh flat-leaf parsley

Slip sharp knife under top of crab shell at back; lever off shell. Remove and discard whitish gills. Rinse well under cold running water. Using cleaver, chop each crab into pieces. Shell and devein prawns, leaving tails intact. Chop fish into 2cm pieces.
Heat oil in large saucepan; cook onion, celery and garlic, stirring, until onion is soft. Add tomato; cook, stirring, 5 minutes or until pulpy. Stir in puree, wine, stock and sugar; simmer, covered, 20 minutes.
Add crab and clams to pan; simmer, covered, 10 minutes (discard any clams that do not open). Add prawns, fish and scallops; cook, stirring occasionally, about 5 minutes or until seafood changes colour and is cooked through. Stir in herbs.

serves 6
per serving 8.6g fat; 1292kJ (309 cal)
tip You can substitute any firm-fleshed fish for the swordfish.

chilli seafood pizza

Use store-bought pizza bases or try making your own.

1 quantity pizza dough
400g uncooked medium prawns
400g squid hoods, sliced thinly
400g cleaned baby octopus, quartered
2 cloves garlic, crushed
1 tablespoon coarsely chopped
 fresh flat-leaf parsley
1 teaspoon sea salt
⅔ cup (180g) bottled tomato
 pasta sauce
4 fresh small red chillies, sliced thinly
4 green onions, sliced thinly
1 medium red onion (170g),
 sliced thinly

Make pizza dough.
Peel and devein prawns. Combine
with squid, octopus, garlic, parsley
and salt in bowl; toss well.
Preheat oven to very hot (240°C/220°C
fan-forced). Lightly oil two 30cm-round
pizza trays. Halve pizza dough. Roll each
piece to 30cm round; place on trays.
Spread bases with tomato sauce.
Divide seafood mixture between pizzas.
Top with chillies and onions. Bake
pizzas 10 minutes. Reduce oven to
moderate (180°C/160°C fan-forced).
Slide pizzas from trays onto oven racks;
bake a further 5 minutes or until crisp.

pizza dough
2 teaspoons (7g) dry yeast
½ teaspoon caster sugar
¾ cup (180ml) warm water
2 cups (300g) plain flour
1 teaspoon salt
2 tablespoons olive oil

Combine yeast, sugar and water in
small bowl; cover, stand in a warm
place about 10 minutes or until
mixture is frothy.
Sift flour and salt into a large bowl;
stir in yeast mixture and olive oil; mix
to a soft dough. Bring dough together
with your hands, add a little extra
water, if necessary.
Knead dough on a lightly floured
surface 10 minutes or until smooth
and elastic. Place in lightly oiled large
bowl; cover, stand in a warm place
about 1 hour or until doubled in size.
Punch dough down; knead on a
lightly floured surface until smooth.

makes 16 slices
per slice 3.4g fat; 615kJ (147 cal)

char-grilled vegetables and polenta with pesto

4 baby eggplants (240g), sliced thickly

2 baby fennel (250g), halved

250g cherry tomatoes

18 baby zucchini (185g)

½ cup (125ml) lemon juice

½ cup (125ml) olive oil

4 cloves garlic, crushed

500g bunch baby beetroot, trimmed

2 cobs of corn (800g), sliced thickly

400g baby carrots, trimmed

350g baby potatoes, halved

¼ cup (65g) bottled pesto

polenta triangles

2½ cups (625ml) water

1 cup (250ml) milk

1½ cups (255g) instant polenta

20g butter

¾ cup (60g) finely grated parmesan

50g seeded black olives, chopped finely

Combine eggplant, fennel, tomatoes and zucchini in large bowl with juice, oil and garlic; cover, refrigerate 3 hours or overnight.

Meanwhile, make polenta triangles.

Preheat oven to moderately hot (200°C/180°C fan-forced). Place beetroot in large oiled baking dish; roast, covered, 15 minutes.

Add corn, carrot and potato to baking dish with beetroot; roast, covered, 30 minutes, turning halfway through cooking.

Peel beetroot. Cook corn, carrot, potato and drained marinated vegetables, in batches, on heated oiled grill plate (or grill or barbecue) until browned and just tender.

Serve vegetables with pesto and polenta triangles.

polenta triangles Heat the water and milk in large saucepan. Add polenta; cook, stirring, about 2 minutes or until liquid is absorbed and mixture thickens. Stir in butter, parmesan and olives. Spoon polenta into 23cm-square slab cake pan, pressing firmly to ensure even thickness; cool to room temperature. Cover; refrigerate about 3 hours or until firm. Turn polenta onto board, trim edges; cut into quarters, cut each quarter into four triangles. Grill polenta on heated oiled grill plate until browned all over.

serves 4

per serving 50g fat; 4122kJ (986 cal)

tip Polenta can be made a day ahead and kept, covered, in the refrigerator.

zabaglione

5 egg yolks
¼ cup (55g) caster sugar
½ cup (125ml) sweet marsala
¼ cup (60ml) dry white wine

Beat yolks and sugar in medium heatproof bowl with electric
mixer until well combined.
Place yolk mixture over medium saucepan of simmering water.
Gradually beat in half of the marsala and half of the wine; beat
well. Gradually beat in remaining marsala and wine.
Beat constantly for about 10 minutes or until mixture is thick
and creamy. If mixture adheres to side of bowl, quickly remove
from heat and beat vigorously with wooden spoon. Pour into
individual dishes; serve immediately.

serves 4
per serving 7.1g fat; 794kJ (190 cal)
tip Zabaglione makes an excellent topping for fresh fruit.

49

tiramisu

2 tablespoons ground espresso coffee
1 cup (250ml) boiling water
½ cup (125ml) marsala
250g packet savoiardi sponge finger biscuits
300ml thickened cream
¼ cup (40g) icing sugar
2 cups (500g) mascarpone
2 tablespoons marsala, extra
50g dark eating chocolate, grated coarsely

Combine coffee and the boiling water in coffee plunger; stand 2 minutes before plunging. Combine coffee mixture and marsala in medium heatproof bowl; cool 10 minutes.

Place a third of the biscuits, in single layer, over base of deep 2-litre (8-cup) dish; drizzle with a third of the coffee mixture.

Beat cream and icing sugar in small bowl until soft peaks form; transfer to large bowl. Fold in combined mascarpone and extra marsala.

Spread a third of the cream mixture over biscuits in dish. Submerge half of the remaining biscuits, one at a time, in coffee mixture, taking care the biscuits do not become so soggy that they fall apart; place over cream layer. Top biscuit layer with half of the remaining cream mixture. Repeat process with remaining biscuits, coffee mixture and cream mixture. Sprinkle with chocolate. Cover; refrigerate 3 hours or overnight.

serves 6
per serving 70.4g fat; 3536kJ (846 cal)

nougat semifreddo with orange and honey syrup

A traditional Italian dessert, semifreddo loosely translates as "a bit cold", and can refer to any partially frozen sweet served at the end of a meal.

1 vanilla bean

3 eggs, separated

⅓ cup (75g) caster sugar

1½ cups (375ml) thickened cream

200g nougat, chopped finely

½ cup (75g) coarsely chopped, toasted shelled pistachios

1 tablespoon honey

orange and honey syrup

¼ cup (90g) honey

1 tablespoon finely grated orange rind

2 tablespoons orange juice

Split vanilla bean in half lengthways; scrape seeds into small bowl, reserve pod for another use. Add yolks and sugar; beat with electric mixer until thick and creamy. Transfer mixture to large bowl.

Beat cream in small bowl with electric mixer until soft peaks form; gently fold cream into yolk mixture.

Beat egg whites in separate small bowl with electric mixer until soft peaks form. Gently fold half of the egg whites into cream mixture; fold in nougat, nuts, honey and remaining egg white. Transfer mixture to 14cm x 21cm loaf pan, cover with foil; freeze 3 hours or until just firm.

Make orange and honey syrup.

Stand semifreddo at room temperature 10 minutes before serving with syrup.

orange and honey syrup Place ingredients in small saucepan; bring to a boil. Reduce heat; simmer, uncovered, 2 minutes.

serves 4
per serving 51.6g fat; 3532kJ (845 cal)

53

clove panna cotta with fresh figs

1 teaspoon whole cloves
300ml thickened cream
⅔ cup (160ml) milk
2 teaspoons gelatine
2 tablespoons caster sugar
½ teaspoon vanilla extract
4 medium fresh figs (240g)
2 tablespoons honey

Grease four ½-cup (125ml) moulds.
Combine cloves, cream and milk in small saucepan; stand 10 minutes. Sprinkle gelatine and sugar over cream mixture; stir over low heat, without boiling, until gelatine and sugar dissolve. Stir in extract. Strain into medium jug; cool to room temperature.
Divide mixture among prepared moulds, cover; refrigerate 3 hours or until set.
Quarter figs; stir honey in small saucepan until warm.
Turn panna cotta out onto serving plates; serve with figs drizzled with honey.

serves 4
per serving 29.3g fat; 1639kJ (392 cal)

panettone bread and butter pudding

Panettone is a sweet Italian yeast bread that can be found at most gourmet delicatessens. Fruit bread can be substituted.

1kg panettone
90g butter, softened
1 litre (4 cups) milk
300ml thickened cream
⅔ cup (150g) caster sugar
1 vanilla bean
3 egg yolks
3 eggs
¼ cup (80g) apricot jam
1 tablespoon orange-flavoured liqueur

Preheat oven to moderately slow (170°C/150°C fan-forced). Grease a deep 22cm-round cake pan; line base and side with baking paper.

Cut panettone in half from top to bottom (reserve half for another use); cut remaining half in half again, then crossways into 1.5cm-thick slices. Toast panettone lightly on both sides; spread one side of each slice with butter while still warm. Slightly overlap panettone slices around edge of pan; layer remaining slices over base of pan.

Combine milk, cream and sugar in medium saucepan. Split vanilla bean in half lengthways; scrape seeds into saucepan, then place pod in saucepan. Stir over heat until mixture boils. Strain into large heatproof jug; discard pod. Cover; cool 10 minutes.

Beat egg yolks and eggs in medium bowl with electric mixer until thick and creamy. Gradually beat in hot milk mixture; pour custard over panettone in pan.

Place pan in large baking dish; add enough boiling water to dish to come halfway up side of pan. Bake, uncovered, about 1½ hours or until custard sets; stand in pan 30 minutes. Carefully turn pudding onto wire rack, then turn top-side up onto serving plate.

Stir jam and liqueur in small saucepan over heat until combined; strain. Brush over warm pudding.

serves 8
per serving 46.9g fat; 3561kJ (852 cal)

lemon gelato

½ cup (110g) caster sugar
½ cup (125ml) water
½ cup (125ml) sweet or dry white wine
½ cup (125ml) lemon juice, strained
1 egg white

Combine sugar, the water and wine in small saucepan; stir over low heat until sugar dissolves. Bring to a boil; reduce heat. Simmer, uncovered, 10 minutes; cool. Stir in juice; mix well. Pour into lamington pan; cover and freeze until just firm.
Remove from freezer. Turn mixture into medium bowl; beat until smooth with fork. Beat egg white in small bowl with electric mixer until firm peaks form; fold into lemon mixture. Return to pan; cover and freeze until firm.

serves 2
per serving 0.1g fat; 1158kJ (277 cal)
tip Gelato is best made a day ahead and can be frozen, covered, for up to 3 days.

glossary

arborio rice small, round grain rice well-suited to absorb a large amount of liquid; especially suitable for risottos.

artichoke hearts tender centre of the globe artichoke, itself the large flower-bud of a member of the thistle family; having tough petal-like leaves, edible in part when cooked. Artichoke hearts can be harvested fresh from the plant or purchased in brine canned or in glass jars.

bacon rashers also known as bacon slices; made from cured and smoked pork side.

beetroot also known as red beets; firm, round root vegetable. Can be eaten raw, grated; boiled and sliced; or roasted then mashed.

breadcrumbs, stale one- or two-day-old bread made into crumbs by grating, blending or processing.

butter use salted or unsalted (sweet) butter; 125g is equal to 1 stick butter.

capers the grey-green buds of a warm climate (usually Mediterranean) shrub, sold either dried and salted or pickled in a vinegar brine; tiny young ones, called baby capers, are also available.

cheese

bocconcini from the diminutive of boccone meaning mouthful, is the term used for walnut-sized, baby mozzarella, a delicate, semi-soft, white cheese traditionally made in Italy from buffalo milk. Spoils rapidly so must be kept under refrigeration, in brine, for 1 or 2 days at most.

fontina a smooth firm cheese with a nutty taste and a brown or red rind.

gorgonzola a creamy Italian blue cheese having a mild, sweet taste; good as an accompaniment to fruit or to flavour sauces etc.

mascarpone a cultured cream product made in much the same way as yogurt. It's whitish to creamy yellow in colour, with a soft, creamy texture.

mozzarella soft, spun-curd cheese; originated in southern Italy where it is traditionally made from water buffalo milk. Cow milk versions of this product, commonly known as pizza cheese, are now available. It has a low melting point and wonderfully elastic texture when heated and is used to add texture rather than flavour.

parmesan also known as parmigiano, parmesan is a hard, grainy cow-milk cheese that originated in the Parma region of Italy. The curd is salted in brine for a month before being aged for up to two years in humid conditions. Parmesan is mainly grated as a topping for pasta, soups and other savoury dishes, but is also delicious eaten with fruit.

pecorino is the generic Italian name for cheeses made from sheep milk. It's a hard, white to pale yellow cheese, traditionally made from November to June when the sheep are grazing on natural pastures. Pecorino is usually matured for eight to

12 months and is known for the region in which it's produced – Romano from Rome, Sardo from Sardinia, Siciliano from Sicily and Toscano from Tuscany.

ricotta soft white cow-milk cheese; roughly translates as "cooked again". It's made from whey, a by-product of other cheese making, to which fresh milk and acid are added. Ricotta is a sweet, moist cheese with a fat content of around 8.5% and a slightly grainy texture.

ciabatta in Italian, the word means "slipper", which is the traditional shape of this popular crisp-crusted white bread.

clams we used a small ridge-shelled variety of this bivalve mollusc; also called vongole.

cloves dried flower buds of a tropical tree; can be used whole or in ground form. Have a strong scent and taste so should be used minimally.

dark eating chocolate made of cocoa liquor, cocoa butter and sugar.

eggplant also known as aubergine; belongs to the same family as tomatoes, chillies and potatoes. Ranging in size from tiny to very large and in colour from pale green to deep purple, eggplant has an equally wide variety of flavours.

eggs some recipes in this book call for raw or barely cooked eggs; exercise caution if there is a salmonella problem in your area.

flour, plain an all-purpose flour, made from wheat.

gelatine we used powdered gelatine; also available in sheet form known as leaf gelatine.

gnocchi Italian "dumplings" made of potatoes, semolina or flour; can be cooked in boiling water or baked with cheese or sauce.

green onions also known as scallions or (incorrectly) shallots; immature onions picked before the bulbs have formed, having long, bright-green edible stalks.

grill, griller broil, broiler.

herbs when specified, we used dried (not ground) herbs in the proportion of one to four for fresh herbs; 1 teaspoon dried herbs equals 4 teaspoons (1 tablespoon) chopped fresh herbs.

parsley, flat-leaf also known as continental or italian parsley.

sage pungent herb with narrow, grey-green leaves; slightly bitter with a slightly musty mint aroma. Refrigerate fresh sage wrapped in a paper towel and sealed in a plastic bag for up to 4 days.

italian salami aged and air-dried, and spiced with garlic and peppercorns.

jam also known as preserve or conserve; most often made from fruit.

lamington pan 20cm x 30cm slab cake pan, 3cm deep.

lasagne sheets, fresh thinly rolled, wide sheets of plain or flavoured pasta not requiring par-boiling prior to being used in cooking. Available in various sizes from most supermarkets.

marinara mix a mixture of uncooked, chopped seafood available from fishmarkets and fishmongers.

milk we used full-cream homogenised milk unless otherwise specified.

mince also known as ground meat.

mustard, dijon a pale brown, distinctively flavoured, fairly mild french mustard.

polenta also known as cornmeal; a flour-like cereal made of dried corn (maize) sold ground in several different textures; also the name of the dish made from it.

rocket also known as arugula, rugula and rucola; a peppery-tasting green leaf that can be used similarly to baby spinach leaves, eaten raw in salad or used in cooking. Baby rocket leaves are both smaller and less peppery.

sugar we used coarse, granulated table sugar, also known as crystal sugar, unless otherwise specified.

caster also known as superfine or finely granulated table sugar.

icing sugar also known as confectioners' sugar or powdered sugar; pulverised granulated sugar crushed together with a small amount (about 3%) cornflour added.

tomatoes

canned whole peeled tomatoes in natural juices.

egg also called plum or roma, these are smallish, oval-shaped tomatoes much used in Italian cooking or salads.

paste triple-concentrated tomato puree used to flavour soups, stews, sauces and casseroles.

puree canned pureed tomatoes (not tomato paste). Substitute with fresh peeled and pureed tomatoes.

vanilla

bean dried, long, thin pod from a tropical golden orchid grown in Central and South America and Tahiti; the minuscule black seeds inside the bean are used to impart a luscious vanilla flavour in baking and desserts. A whole bean can be placed in the sugar container to make the vanilla sugar often called for in recipes.

extract obtained from vanilla beans infused in water. A non-alcoholic version of essence. Vanilla essence is not a suitable substitute.

veal osso buco another name used by butchers for veal shin, usually cut into 3cm- to 5cm-thick slices and used in the famous Italian slow-cooked casserole of the same name.

wonton wrappers also known as wonton skins; made of flour, eggs and water, they come in varying thicknesses. Sold packaged in large amounts and found in the refrigerated section of Asian grocery stores; gow gee, egg or spring roll pastry sheets can be substituted.

zucchini also known as courgette. A member of the squash family. Also has edible flowers.

index

facts & figures

These conversions are approximate only, but the difference between an exact and the approximate conversion of various liquid and dry measures is minimal and will not affect your cooking results.

Note: NZ, Canada, US and UK all use 15ml tablespoons. Australian tablespoons measure 20ml. All cup and spoon measurements are level.

Measuring equipment
The difference between one country's measuring cups and another's is, at most, within a 2 or 3 teaspoon variance. (For the record, 1 Australian metric measuring cup holds approximately 250ml.) The most accurate way of measuring dry ingredients is to weigh them. For liquids, use a clear glass or plastic jug having metric markings.

How to measure
When using graduated measuring cups, shake dry ingredients loosely into the appropriate cup. Do not tap the cup on a bench or tightly pack the ingredients unless directed to do so. Level the top of measuring cups and measuring spoons with a knife. When measuring liquids, place a clear glass or plastic jug having metric markings on a flat surface to check accuracy at eye level.

Dry measures

metric	imperial
15g	½oz
30g	1oz
60g	2oz
90g	3oz
125g	4oz (¼lb)
155g	5oz
185g	6oz
220g	7oz
250g	8oz (½lb)
280g	9oz
315g	10oz
345g	11oz
375g	12oz (¾lb)
410g	13oz
440g	14oz
470g	15oz
500g	16oz (1lb)
750g	24oz (1½lb)
1kg	32oz (2lb)

We use large eggs with an average weight of 60g.

Liquid measures

metric	imperial
30 ml	1 fluid oz
60 ml	2 fluid oz
100 ml	3 fluid oz
125 ml	4 fluid oz
150 ml	5 fluid oz (¼ pint/1 gill)
190 ml	6 fluid oz
250 ml (1cup)	8 fluid oz
300 ml	10 fluid oz (½ pint)
500 ml	16 fluid oz
600 ml	20 fluid oz (1 pint)
1000 ml (1litre)	1¾ pints

Helpful measures

metric	imperial
3mm	⅛in
6mm	¼in
1cm	½in
2cm	¾in
2.5cm	1in
6cm	2½in
8cm	3in
20cm	8in
23cm	9in
25cm	10in
30cm	12in (1ft)

Oven temperatures
These oven temperatures are only a guide for conventional ovens. For fan-forced ovens, check the manufacturer's manual.

	°C (Celsius)	°F (Fahrenheit)	Gas Mark
Very slow	120	250	½
Slow	150	275-300	1-2
Moderately slow	170	325	3
Moderate	180	350-375	4-5
Moderately hot	200	400	6
Hot	220	425-450	7-8
Very hot	240	475	9

Are you missing some of the world's favourite cookbooks?

The Australian Women's Weekly cookbooks are available from bookshops, cookshops, supermarkets and other stores all over the world. You can also buy direct from the publisher, using the order form below.

MINI SERIES £2.50 190x138MM 64 PAGES

TITLE	QTY	TITLE	QTY	TITLE	QTY
4 Fast Ingredients		Crumbles & Bakes		Noodles	
15-minute Feasts		Curries		Outdoor Eating	
30-minute Meals		Drinks		Party Food	
50 Fast Chicken Fillets		Fast Fish		Pasta	
After-work Stir-fries		Fast Food for Friends		Pickles and Chutneys	
Barbecue		Fast Soup		Potatoes	
Barbecue Chicken		Finger Food		Risotto	
Barbecued Seafood		Gluten-free Cooking		Roast	
Biscuits, Brownies & Biscotti		Healthy Food 4 Kids		Salads	
Bites		Ice-creams & Sorbets		Simple Slices	
Bowl Food		Indian Cooking		Simply Seafood	
Burgers, Rösti & Fritters		Indonesian Favourites		Skinny Food	
Cafe Cakes		Italian		Stir-fries	
Cafe Food		Italian Favourites		Summer Salads	
Casseroles		Jams & Jellies		Tapas, Antipasto & Mezze	
Char-grills & Barbecues		Kids Party Food		Thai Cooking	
Cheesecakes, Pavlovas & Trifles		Last-minute Meals		Thai Favourites	
Chinese Favourites		Lebanese Cooking		Vegetarian	
Chocolate Cakes		Malaysian Favourites		Vegetarian Stir-fries	
Christmas Cakes & Puddings		Mince		Vegie Main Meals	
Cocktails		Muffins		Wok	
				TOTAL COST	£

Photocopy and complete coupon below

Name _____

Address _____

_____ Postcode _____

Country _____ Phone (business hours) _____

Email* (optional) _____
*By including your email address, you consent to receipt of any email regarding this magazine, and other emails which inform you of ACP's other publications, products, services and events, and to promote third party goods and services you may be interested in.

I enclose my cheque/money order for £ _____

or please charge £ _____ to my:

☐ Bankcard ☐ Mastercard ☐ Visa ☐ American Express ☐ Diners Club

Card number ☐☐☐☐☐☐☐☐☐☐☐☐☐☐☐☐☐☐

Cardholder's signature _____ Expiry date ____ /____

To order: Mail or fax – photocopy or complete the order form above, and send your credit card details or cheque payable to: Australian Consolidated Press (UK), Moulton Park Business Centre, Red House Road, Moulton Park, Northampton NN3 6AQ; phone (+44) (01) 604 497531, fax (+44) (01) 604 497533, email books@acpmedia.co.uk. Or order online at www.acpuk.com
Non-UK residents: We accept the credit cards listed on the coupon, or cheques, drafts or International Money Orders payable in sterling and drawn on a UK bank. Credit card charges are at the exchange rate current at the time of payment.
Postage and packing UK: Add £1.00 per order plus 25p per book.
Postage and packing overseas: Add £2.00 per order plus 50p per book.
Offer ends 30.06.2006